THE LION

First Book *of*
Parables

To my lovely Dad   B.V.

Text by Lois Rock
Illustrations copyright © 2014 Barbara Vagnozzi
This edition copyright © 2014 Lion Hudson

Published by Lion Children's Books
an imprint of
Lion Hudson plc
Wilkinson House, Jordan Hill Road,
Oxford OX2 8DR, England
www.lionhudson.com/lionchildrens

ISBN 978 0 7459 6409 6

First edition 2014

A catalogue record for this book is available from the British Library

Printed and bound in China, December 2013, LH17

The Lion
First Book of Parables

RETOLD BY LOIS ROCK
ILLUSTRATED BY BARBARA VAGNOZZI

LION
CHILDREN'S

Contents

The Sower

It was a day like so many others. Jesus went down to the beach on Lake Galilee and began to preach.

In no time at all a large crowd gathered. Others arrived and tried to squeeze their way closer to the front. Jesus found himself being inched closer to the lapping water. Too close, in fact.

Jesus climbed onto a friend's boat and asked for it to be floated a little way into the lake. There he had both space and dry feet.

There everyone could see him. He began to tell stories to help explain his message: parables.

"There was once a farmer who went out to sow his field," said Jesus. "He walked up and down the rows of ploughed earth flinging handfuls of seeds from his basket.

"Some seeds fell on the path. Almost at once birds came swooping down and pecked them up.

"Some fell on rocky ground. The seeds soon sprouted, even though the soil was thin. As the season wore on, the sun grew hotter. The roots could not grow any deeper to find water, and the plants wilted and died.

"Some seeds fell among thorn bushes. They soon uncurled their first leaves, but they could not reach the light. The young plants drooped and died, choked by the taller plants around them.

"Other seeds fell on good soil. They grew into tall, strong plants. They were the ones that bore a good harvest of grain: some a hundred, others sixty, others thirty.

"And this is the message: listen, if you have ears to hear."
But did anyone have the wisdom they needed? Jesus' own close friends and companions, the disciples, were puzzled.
"Why do you use parables to talk to the people?" they asked.
"Not everyone is going to understand my message," replied Jesus. "It is only for those who want to be part of the God's kingdom.
"Let me explain the story:

"The seeds that fell on the path are those who hear my words but not the message. The Evil One snatches my words from their minds.

"The seeds that fell on rocky soil are the eager ones. My preaching gets them all fired up to follow me, but as soon as the going gets tough, they give up.

"The seeds that fell among thorns are the half-hearted. They like my preaching, but they make only a feeble attempt to obey it. Everyday worries keep on getting in the way.

"The seeds that fell in good soil are those that hear my message and understand it. As a result, they live good and fruitful lives."

The Hidden Treasure

Jesus often spoke about something he called "the kingdom of heaven". But what is it?

"The kingdom is like this," said Jesus.

"A man is digging in a farmer's field. It's just an everyday job… and it's hard work.

"All of a sudden, his spade hits a stone. Wouldn't you know it! Now he'll have to scrabble to shift the earth around it.

"There he is, on his hands and knees, up to his ears in dirt.

"But wait. It isn't a stone.

It's… *treasure!*

"Imagine how quickly he fills in that hole. Then he goes home and sells everything he owns so he has enough money to buy the entire field."

The Finest Pearl in the World

What is God's kingdom like? Jesus told this story.

"There was once a merchant who traded in pearls:
large pearls, small pearls;
cream pearls, pink pearls;
white pearls, black pearls;
sea pearls, river pearls…

"Oh yes, that man knew his pearls. But whatever the type of pearl he went looking for, he only ever bought the best.

"One day, almost by chance, he came across someone who was offering – so he claimed – the most wonderful pearl.

"The merchant looked just ever so slightly bored as the seller unwrapped the promised item. He knew that anyone who looks too eager to buy will be asked a high price. And then he saw it.

"Surely it was the *finest* pearl in the world. Ever.

"He just had to have it. Whatever it cost.

"So he did what he had to do. He went and sold his entire stock of pearls and came back to buy the one that really was priceless."

13

The Mustard Seed

"The kingdom of God," said Jesus, "is like this.

"A man takes a tiny mustard seed and sows it in his field.

"To a passer-by, it might look like nothing has happened there.

"Even so, the seed will wake and grow.

"Season by season it will grow into a tree.

"All kinds of birds will come and make their nests among its branches."

The Great Feast

Jesus had been invited to a banquet.

"This is a real treat," said the person sitting at the table with him. "But it is those who sit down to eat in God's kingdom who will be truly blessed."

Jesus replied with a story.

"There was once a man who was giving a great feast. He sent his invitations far and wide and began to make elaborate preparations.

"At last the day came.

"'Hurry,' he told his servant. 'Take messages to all the people I invited. Tell them that everything is ready… and remind them to be on time.'

"The servant went, expecting to be greeted with smiles and cheers.

"To his dismay, people began making excuses.

"'I've just bought a field. I need to go and look at it.'

"'I've bought five ox teams. I must go and try them out.'

"'I've just got married. I'm far too busy now!'

"When the servant went back and reported that **EVERYONE** had made an excuse, the man was furious.

" 'Ungrateful scoundrels!' he roared. 'They'll be sorry for this.'

"Then he calmed down a little.

" 'I want you to go out a second time,' he said. 'Forget the ungrateful lot.

" 'Go into the poorer streets of the town and invite all the poor people and those who are so disabled they can only beg for a living.'

"The servant did so and many came.

" 'There is still room for more,' he told his master.
   " 'Then go out into the country lanes and tracks and find other people who are willing to come,' said the man.
   " 'I want my house to be full.' "

The Lost Sheep

The old men scowled at the crowds hurrying toward Jesus.
"I see a rather large number of tax collectors," sniffed one.
"Along with other cheats and lowlifes," added a second.
"Jesus can't be up to much if he wants followers like these."
Jesus began telling a story.

"There was once a shepherd who had a hundred sheep.

"They knew the sound of his voice, and they followed him eagerly when he led them to where the grass grew lush and green.

"One day, when he reached a new pasture, he turned to count them.

"To his dismay, he could only see ninety-nine.

"He counted again. No, there was no mistake.

"*One of the sheep was missing.*

"He waved to some village children who were playing nearby. 'Hey, can you keep an eye on this lot of sheep? There's one missing. I need to go and find it.'

"While the ninety-nine sheep munched happily in the pasture, the shepherd set off over the hills.

"Carefully he retraced his path, stopping every now and then to call his shepherd's cry.

"At last he heard the sound he had been listening for: a high, sorrowful bleat.

"He hurried over a tumble of boulders and thorn bushes to find his lost sheep.

" 'There you are!'

"Gently he picked it up and lifted it on to his shoulders.

"Then, as the sun slowly set, he carried the sheep back home. There was just time to drive the flock safely into the fold: all one hundred of them safe at last.

"Then he called to all his friends.
" 'Time to celebrate!' he said. 'I found my lost sheep.
'Let's have a party.'

"In the same way," said Jesus,
"there is more joy in heaven
when just one wrongdoer mends
their ways than over ninety-nine
respectable people who have always
stayed on the straight and narrow."

The Workers in the Vineyard

"This story is about the grape harvest," said Jesus. "And it's about a man who needed some extra workers to gather the fruit from his vineyard.

"Well, he got up early and went to the marketplace to find out who was available for casual work. He found some lads already lining up in the usual place and offered them a silver coin for the day's wage. They were delighted and set off at once.

"The lads had done a lot of picking fruit and filling baskets and taking them off to the wine press when nine o'clock rolled around.

"The vineyard owner hurried back to the marketplace. Surely some more people would have turned up for work now? Ah yes! More strong lads looking hopeful.

"'Work in my vineyard today and I guarantee you a fair wage,' said the man.

"The lads all trooped off and joined the others.

"At noon, when the sun was hot, the vineyard owner made a third trip to the marketplace. There were yet more people standing idle, wondering if there might be any jobs going that day.

"'Come with me,' he called to them. 'I pay fair wages.'

"The same thing happened at three o'clock, and again at five the man went back to the marketplace. Astonishingly, there were still people lining up for jobs.

" 'Why are you here hanging around?' cried the vineyard owner. 'Don't you care that you'll waste a whole day doing nothing?'

" 'No one has offered us a job,' came the moping reply.

" 'Well, I'm offering you a job right now,' said the man. 'Come with me to the vineyard. I need all the hands I can get.'

"When evening came, the vineyard owner gave instructions to his foreman.

" 'It's time to pay the workers their wages,' he said. 'Start with those men I hired last, and so on until you get to the ones I hired first.'

"So the foreman called out. 'Five o'clock starters, over here, please.' He gave each of them a silver coin.

"Next he paid the three o'clock starters, then the twelve o'clock starters and the nine o'clock starters.

"By this time, the early morning starters had seen those who were paid first dancing off gleefully each with their silver coin.

"'We're in for some decent money today,' they agreed among themselves, and they jumped up eagerly when it was their turn to go up to the foreman.

"He gave each of them a silver coin.

"'What's this about?' they complained. 'We've been hard at work for hours, right through the heat of the day. How do you explain giving us no more than those scroungers who turned up at five and put in one hour?'

"The vineyard owner hurried over to explain.

"'I'm not cheating you,' he said. 'I'm paying you exactly what you agreed to.

"'Take your pay and go.

"'I have a right to do as I like with my money. I think you're jealous that I'm generous.'

"And this is why I told the story," said Jesus. "In the kingdom of God, the last will be first, and the first will be last."

The Two Sons

"Once," said Jesus, "there was a man who had two sons.

"He went to the elder one. 'Son, I want you to go and work in the vineyard today,' he said.

"'No way!' came the grumbling reply.

"So the man went to his younger son and asked the same thing.

"'Of course I'll go,' came the cheerful reply.

"But the younger son didn't go. He'd just said what the father wanted to hear.

"Meanwhile, the elder son began to feel bad about his oafish behaviour. Without saying a word, he went to the vineyard to do whatever needed to be done.

"In the same way," added Jesus, "some people say they want to be part of God's kingdom, but they do not change their ways as they should."

The Cunning Servant

Jesus told his disciples this story.

"There was once a very wealthy man. It was a huge job to make sure that everything he owned was properly looked after. What he needed was to find a loyal servant who could do the work for him.

"He chose someone who seemed trustworthy and turned his attention to other things. For a while all seemed well. Then someone brought bad news.

" 'I think you ought to check what your servant is up to,' said the messenger. 'The word on the street is that he's wasting your money willy-nilly. Either he's a scoundrel or he's not up to the job.'

"The wealthy man acted at once and demanded a meeting with the servant.

" 'What's this I hear about your management?' he roared.

31

" 'I want you to prepare a full statement of what you've been doing. If I find anything I don't like, you'll be out of a job in an instant.'

"The servant was dismayed.

" 'I'm going to be fired,' he wailed to himself. 'Whatever shall I do after that?

" 'I'm not strong enough to dig ditches any more. And I'm too ashamed to beg.'

"Then he had an idea.

" 'I know! I'll use the time I still have in the job to make friends. Then they will give me a welcome and a place to stay when I really need it.'

"He arranged to meet all the people who owed his master money.

" 'How much do you owe?' he asked the first one.

" 'One hundred barrels of olive oil,' came the reply.

" 'Really?' said the servant. 'That's far too much. It must be a mistake I made. Take this statement of your account and change the 100 to 50.'

"The olive oil woman was delighted.

So the servant called the next person in.

" 'How much do you owe?' he asked him.

" 'A thousand sacks of wheat,' came the reply.

" 'Really?' said the servant. 'That's far too much. It must be a mistake I made. Take this statement of your account and change 1000 to 800.'

"And so it went on: everyone who owed the wealthy man money was given a hefty write-down. They were all very, very grateful.

"When the wealthy man found out what had happened, he simply laughed.

"'You're a cunning one, and no mistake,' he told the servant. 'I can see you have a very good understanding of how to make money work in business.'

The disciples looked a little puzzled.

"This is the lesson of the story," Jesus explained. "Use worldly wealth wisely, to make friends.

"When the money runs out – as it most certainly will – you will be welcomed into heaven.

"Only those who can be trusted with worldly wealth have the wisdom to handle true wealth.

"You cannot serve both God and money."

The Rich Man and Lazarus

"Beware of the lure of money," warned Jesus. "The things that humans value are worth nothing in God's sight."

He told this story.

"There was once a man so rich he could buy everything he wanted: the clothes, the house, the lifestyle. Everything he had was of the most luxurious.

"A poor man named Lazarus came and sat outside his property every day. All he hoped for was some of the kitchen scraps. The dogs that were also waiting for some leftovers used to lick the sores on Lazarus' body.

"Well, the poor man died and the angels carried him to heaven, to feast at the table of the great prophet Abraham.

"The rich man also died but he went to the other place – the place of fire and torment.

"As he looked up, he saw the wonderful party in heaven.

"'Father Abraham,' he called. 'Please help. Please send Lazarus with the tiniest bit of water for me. I'm dying of thirst down here.'

"Abraham looked down sternly.

"'In life you had all the good things that money can buy,' he said. 'Lazarus had none.

"'This is the result. I'm afraid it can't be changed now.'

"'Oh dear,' wailed the rich man. 'Then let me beg just one thing. Send someone to warn my five brothers of what lies ahead. They still have time to mend their ways.'

"'The prophets of old have given them warning enough,' snapped Abraham. 'It's all there in the holy books.'

"'But they don't know how important it is to pay attention,' replied the rich man. 'They need someone to rise from the dead and tell them exactly what they face.'

"Abraham shook his head. 'If they haven't listened to the prophets, they won't listen even if someone does rise from the dead.'"

The Two Men at the Temple

"Take care not to look down on others," warned Jesus. And he told this story.

"There were once two men who went to the Temple to pray.

"One was very religious. He belonged to the group called the Pharisees."

They are sticklers for keeping to the rules. In fact they have rules about what's right and wrong for everything – it's frightening.

"Anyway, the Pharisee stood up and said this:

"'O God, I thank you that I am able to keep myself apart from wrongdoing. I am not greedy, I am never dishonest, and I wouldn't dream of being unfaithful. I fast two days a week and I give a tenth of all my income to charity.

"'How different my life is from that of the tax collector over there.'

"The tax collector was indeed 'over there', at the back, on his knees.

"He knew he'd bent quite a few rules in his time, and broken a few more.

"'O God, have pity on me, a sinner,' he said.

"And for that prayer," said Jesus, "it was the tax collector who went home at peace with God."

The Widow and the Judge

"When you pray," said Jesus, "be of good heart. Never get discouraged.

"In one particular town, the local judge was a rascal. He had no respect for God or for his fellow human beings. Were people being treated fairly? What did he care?

"Now, in that town there was a widow who had been cheated by a local scoundrel.

"She went and put her case to the judge. 'I need your help to sort out the dispute fairly,' she pleaded.

"'Of course,' he said absent-mindedly. 'I'll look into it.'

"The widow waited. She heard nothing. She went back to the judge.

" 'Ah, your little case,' he said. 'I seem to have overlooked it. Give me a little longer.'

"The widow waited. She heard nothing. She went back.

" 'I still need your help with my dispute,' she said.

" 'Of course,' said the judge. He did nothing.

"Back came the widow. Again. And again. And again.

" 'I'll have to do something,' the judge decided. 'That woman is wearing me out.'

"For that reason, the widow got the justice she deserved.

"So if a hopeless judge will do that," said Jesus, "how much more will God listen to those who pray to him day and night?"

The Friend at Midnight

Jesus spent time every day saying prayers to God.

"Teach us to pray," his disciples asked.

Jesus told them the words to know by heart. Then he told this story.

"Imagine it's the end of a long day. You are settling cosily into your bed when…

rat tat tat

"There comes a knock at the door.

"Warily you head downstairs. Who could be calling at this late hour?

"It's an old friend! You haven't met up in ever such a long time. He's on a journey. Could he stay at your house overnight?

"'Of course!'

"You welcome him indoors… but then remember…

"You have nothing to offer by way of a meal. But maybe your friend next door has.

"So what do you do? You go and knock on their door.

rat tat tat

RAT TAT TAT

RAT TAT TAT

"At last you get a response.

"'What do you think you're doing?' comes the shout. It's an angry response.

"'I've got a surprise visitor,' you call back. 'I'm out of food. Can you let me have some bread?'

"'Don't bother me at this time of night,' grumbles your friend. 'We're all in bed and we're not getting up.'

"But you really need some bread. So what do you do?

"You knock again. And again. And again.

"In the end your friend does come down and gives you all the bread you could possibly want.

"You get what you needed because you weren't ashamed to go on asking.

"So remember this when you pray:
"Ask, and you will receive.
Seek, and you will find.
Knock, and the door will be opened to you."

Building a Tower

Wherever Jesus went, great crowds gathered behind him.

He turned and spoke to them. "Think hard about how much you want to be my followers," he said. "You will have to give up everything, maybe even your life.

"You would think hard if you were planning to build a tower. You would sit down and work out the cost.

"After all, if you started a grand project like that and ran out of money, wouldn't everyone jeer and mock?

"'Look! There's the man who couldn't finish his own job.

"'What foolishness.'"

The Unforgiving Servant

One day, a disciple came to Jesus with this question:

"If someone does me wrong, how many times should I forgive him? Seven times, perhaps?"

"Not seven," replied Jesus, "rather, seventy times seven.

"The kingdom of God is like this:

"There was once a king who decided to check on how much money he had.

"Almost at once, he discovered something he had overlooked.

"One of his servants owed him a huge amount of money. Worse, he showed no sign of ever paying it back.

"He asked to see the man. 'You must pay me back at once,' said the king.

"'I'm sorry, Your Majesty,' the man replied. 'I simply don't have the cash.'

"'Don't have the cash!' roared the king. 'Then you'll pay your debt a different way.'

"He snapped his fingers toward his right-hand man. 'Sell this man as a slave,' he ordered. 'Sell his wife and children as well.'

"The man fell on his knees.

"*'Please no!*

"'Show me some pity,' he said. 'Wait a little longer. I'm sure I can get the money together if you give me time.'

"The king sighed.

"'All right, off you go,' he said.

"To his right-hand man he added, 'I sometimes think I'm too soft-hearted.'

"The man who had been let off his debt went away, thinking hard about how to get the money together.

"He saw a fellow servant passing by and remembered something useful.

" 'You owe me money,' he growled, as he grabbed the poor unfortunate by the neck. 'I need it now.'

" 'Show some pity,' wailed the unfortunate servant. 'It's only a small amount. Please would you wait a little longer? I'm sure I can get the money together if you give me time.'

" 'I'm not waiting,' said the man. 'You deserve to be punished for this.'

"And he ordered the servant to be thrown into jail.

"The other servants were upset when they found out what had happened. They went and told the king. He called in the first servant.

" 'You worthless slave,' roared the king. 'I showed you pity, and for that reason alone you should have shown pity.

" 'But you didn't. So now it's you who will go to prison until you pay me back everything.'

"And that," said Jesus, "is how God will treat you unless you truly forgive."

The Two House Builders

"There are two sorts of people," said Jesus. "Those who learn from what I say and those who don't.

"Now here's a story about two builders.

"One thought really hard about location. He chose a place high on a rock. It was hard work getting all the stuff he needed up to the site, but he thought it was worth it. In the end he got it all done.

"Not long after, a great storm blew in.
The rain poured down and the wind howled.

whoooooo

"The builder was safe and snug indoors.
"The other builder had his house done much more quickly.
He'd chosen a lovely flat piece of ground right next to the
river.
"Did he care as the rain poured down?
"He did not.
"But the rain made the river overflow.
When the wind roared…

whaaaaa

"… his house fell flat."

The Three Servants

"The kingdom of heaven," said Jesus, "will be like this.

"A man was about to set out on a long journey.

"Before he left, he called his servants.

"'I am going to give each of you some of my property,' he said. 'I want you to look after it while I'm away.

"'The amount you get will depend on how able I think you are to manage the job.'

"He gave one servant five thousand gold coins; another, two thousand gold coins; the third, one thousand gold coins.

"The servant who had been given five thousand gold coins was full of ideas about what to do. Perhaps he should invest it in a vineyard? Or a pottery workshop? Or as a merchant in fine fabrics?

"At last the servant chose and he set up his business.

"The second servant was a little bit scared of the challenges that lay ahead.

" 'I think I might just have a market stall,' he decided. 'I used to help granny with hers. I think I could make that work.'

"The third servant stacked up his thousand gold coins in little piles. He counted them over and over. One thousand. All bright and shiny.

"Ooh – what if someone stole them? That would be the worst thing ever.

"He went out into the garden, dug a hole, and buried the coins his master had given him.

"After a long time the master returned. He called his servants and asked about the money.

"The first came in smiling. 'You gave me five thousand coins,' he said. 'I've used it to earn another five thousand.'

"'Well done!' said the master. 'You are a good and faithful servant. Now I'm back, I'm going to put you in charge of even larger sums of money.'

"The second came in with a shy grin.

"'You gave me two thousand coins,' he said. 'I've used it to earn another two thousand.'

"'Well done!' said the master. 'You are a good and faithful servant. Now I'm back, I'm going to put you in charge of even larger sums of money.'

"Then the servant who had been given one thousand coins came in trembling.

" 'Sir, I knew you were a demanding man,' he said.

" 'I was afraid to lose your money, so I hid it in the ground. I have kept it all absolutely safe until now.'

"The master frowned. 'You lazy good-for-nothing.

" 'You could at the very least have put my money in the bank. That way I might have earned some interest on it.'

"He turned to another servant.

" 'Take this man's coins and give them to the one who has ten thousand.

" 'To every person who has made something of their gifts, more will be given.

" 'The person who has made nothing will lose the little they have.' "

Building Barns for a Bumper Harvest

"Don't spend your life trying to get rich," Jesus told his listeners. "There are much more important things to care about."

And he told this story.

"There was once a farmer who was actually not fretting about the harvest.

"'The soil here is rich and fertile,' he told everyone. 'I get great crops, year after year.'

"The other farmers could only agree. 'That's how he made his money,' they grumbled among themselves. 'Some people have all the luck.'

"Curiously, the wealthy farmer was not without worries.

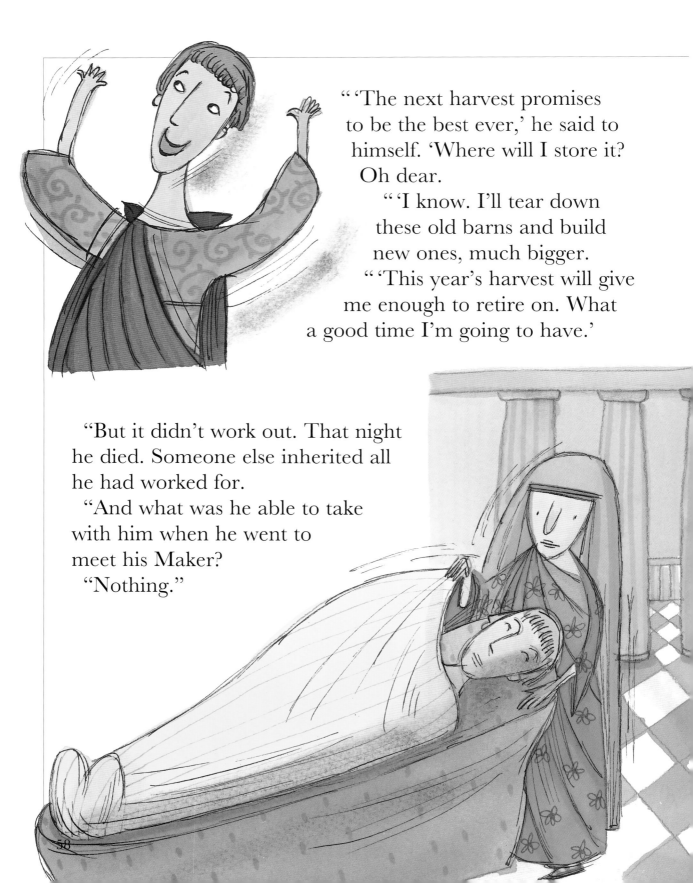

" 'The next harvest promises to be the best ever,' he said to himself. 'Where will I store it? Oh dear.

" 'I know. I'll tear down these old barns and build new ones, much bigger.

" 'This year's harvest will give me enough to retire on. What a good time I'm going to have.'

"But it didn't work out. That night he died. Someone else inherited all he had worked for.

"And what was he able to take with him when he went to meet his Maker?

"Nothing."

A Tale of Two Servants

"You must always be ready," Jesus told his disciples. "You never know when God will come to claim his kingdom.

"There was once a wealthy man who had to go on a long journey. He chose one of his servants to run the household while he was away. The servant knew exactly what was expected of him.

"Everything was kept in perfect order.

"Everyone got treated fairly.

"Every penny was wisely spent.

"When the master returned, he was delighted.

"'I'm going to put you in charge of all my property,' he said.

"But another wealthy man made a poor choice.

"The servant he put in charge of his household behaved perfectly well when his master was watching.

"When his master was gone, he proved to be lazy and selfish.

"He beat the servants for the slightest mistake.

"He helped himself to the wine cellar and invited fellow drinkers around for one long party.

"The wealthy man returned unannounced. He was appalled at what he found, and threw the good-for-nothing out."

The Ten Bridesmaids

"When God's kingdom comes," said Jesus, "it will be like this.

"It was the day of a big wedding. The bride was at home getting ready for the ceremony.

"The bridegroom and his friends were expected to arrive in the early evening.

"The ten bridesmaids went out ready to greet him. Each of them had a lamp to light the last few steps of his way to meet his bride.

"The evening sun sank beneath the horizon. The sky turned dark. Ten little flames burned merrily in the night.

"But the night wore on. A thin moon glimmered silver. A few stars shone. One by one, each of the ten girls put down their lamps, and settled down for just a little snooze.

"All of a sudden, a cry rang out.

"'Here comes the bridegroom!' And a merry party of young men came whooping and singing along the road.

"'Oh, help!' gasped the bridesmaids. 'Our lamps have burned really low.

"'Quick, pull out a bit more of the wick to get a bigger flame.'

"As they did so, they noticed something else: the oil in their lamps had nearly burned away.

"'Add some more in the top,' said the eldest bridesmaid firmly. 'Use the spare oil you brought.'

"Four more bridesmaids reached for tiny bottles and did as she said. The other five began to wail.

"*'Oooh noooo!*

"'We forgot to bring any extra oil.'

" 'Our lamps are going out.'

" 'Can we have some of yours?'

"The five who had brought extra shook their heads glumly. 'We've only got enough for our own lamps,' they said. 'You'll have to go and get some more.'

"So the five forgetful ones hurried off.

"While they were gone, the bridegroom arrived to five welcoming lights.

"The door of the house was flung wide and everyone trooped in to begin the celebrations.

"When the other five came back, the door was locked.

bang bang

" 'Let us in!' they cried.
"The bridegroom looked out. 'I don't think I know you,' he said. 'Goodbye.'
"So remember," said Jesus. "Always be ready for God's kingdom. It might come any day, any time."